28 Ways to
Influence People
& Gain "Buy In"

By Doug Staneart

28 WAYS TO INFLUENCE PEOPLE

ISBN: 978-0-9818257-1-7

DOUG STANEART

Why this Book was Written...

Since 2002, The Leader's Institute® instructors have developed and refined processes that help people communicate with, lead, and motivate others more effectively. At the beginning of each High Impact Leaders ™ program, class members are given a desktop card file with 28 Leadership Principles and are asked to purposefully apply **one principle a day for the next 28 days**.

This book was created to offer **real life examples of each principle**. If you purposefully apply these principles in your life, I think you will be surprised at the number of people you will influence in a positive way. To get the best results, **look for ways to apply one principle per day for 28 consecutive days**.

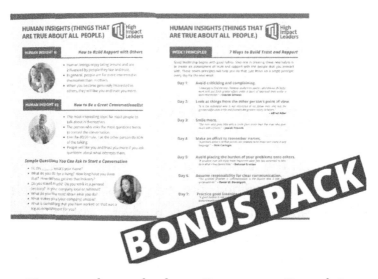

Download the Bonus Pack!

- Download the FREE High Impact Leaders BONUS PACK from leadersinstitute.com/bonuspack
- Get a summary of all the important tips in the book.
- Get eight (8) additional "Human Insight" lists that help you motivate, persuade, and influence other people. (These tips are NOT in the book!)

Week #1: Build Trust and Rapport with the People that You Want to Lead.

Think about the relationships that you have with others as being a checking account. Each person that you interact with has an entirely different account. When we have positive interactions with a person, we make deposits into that account.

However, when something negative occurs or there is a conflict, a withdrawal is made. So, if you want to build trust in a team, you as the leader must make a tremendous number of deposits into the accounts of each team member.

Below are seven ways to build trust within a team. We suggest that you spend a week focusing on a single principle every day. Don't go to bed each day before you apply the principle for that day. By the

1

end of the week, you should already begin to see significant changes in the rapport that you have with others.

1. Avoid Criticizing Your Team.
2. Look at Things from the Other Person's Point of View.
3. Smile More. (It Makes You More Approachable and Friendly.)
4. Make an Effort to Remember Names.
5. Avoid Placing the Burdens of Your Problems onto Your Team's Shoulders.
6. Take Responsibility for Clear Communication.
7. Practice Good Listening Skills.

Leadership Principle #1

Avoid Criticizing and Complaining

"I have yet to find the man, however exalted his station, who did not do better work and put forth greater effort under a spirit of approval than under a spirit of criticism." **– Charles Schwab**

My college football team had an offensive coordinator who was arguably one of the most brilliant minds in the game. However, he used fear and criticism to motivate his players.

If someone missed a block, he'd yell and curse. If a player dropped a pass, he'd shout profanities and ridicule the player.

Consequently, the players were focusing on their **mistakes** rather than their successes. The coach eventually moved on, and after he left, morale improved dramatically. The very next year, the team won their first bowl game in years and went on to twelve straight bowl games in the following years.

The practices were the same. The fan support was the same. The only thing that changed was the atmosphere on the field during the practices and the games.

WHAT MAKES A GREAT LEADER?

Think about someone who you know who you think is a great leader. Is this the type of person who quibbles and complains about irrelevant issues? Does the person point out every mistake? Probably not. In fact, this person probably does just the opposite. The person is probably a master at keeping others focused on the relevant and pointing out every improvement.

ANY JERK CAN COMPLAIN

Any jerk can complain or criticize – and most do. But real leaders are the people who build others up, not tear them down.

Typically, when we point out mistakes that others are making, we are doing so to create a behavior change in the person. However, when we point out mistakes that others make, the automatic human reaction is to get defensive or shift blame elsewhere.

People rarely make a change in their behavior based on criticism.

In section three, we'll cover seven ways to create behavior change in others without raising resentment. Each of these tips will work much better than constructive criticism.

The next time you feel like you need to complain or to criticize someone, think about the outcome you want. Do you want that person to change his behavior? If so, by criticizing, you will cause the person to want to defend himself. This booklet is full of principles that you can use to build trust with and ultimately influence others. The next time you want to criticize or complain, try silence as an option.

Week #1: Build Trust and Rapport Quickly
Principle #1: Avoid Criticizing and Complaining

Leadership Principle #2

Look at Things from the Other Person's Point of View

"It is the individual who is not interested in his fellow men who has the greatest difficulties in life and provides the greatest injury to others."
– Alfred Adler

One of the most primary desires of human beings is to be understood and esteemed by others. We want people to see things from our point of view. Sometimes we want this so badly, that we disagree with and argue with points of view that are also valid.

A business owner I know hired a young man who, in his first year, broke all of the sales records for the company. This young man had fantastic ideas that would revolutionize the way the company sold its services. The owner was very cautious about implementing these ideas, though. He had spent years building his company and was very careful about making changes.

The salesman debated and eventually argued with his boss, and the boss, after being backed into a corner, argued back. Neither had the courage or the foresight to take a step back and try to see things from the other person's point of view.

The frustrated salesman finally gave up a promising career and quit. The boss lost a great salesperson, because neither took the time to understand the other.

A LOT OF DISAGREEMENTS COME FROM REFUSING TO SEE THINGS FROM THE OTHER'S PERSPECTIVE

This very thing happens day after day in businesses and families around the world. Human nature is that we always believe that we are right. Guess what? The other guy thinks the same thing. So, if you dig your heels in, he will dig in his heels as well. All that we have to do is take a step back and say, "Why is this person thinking the way that he is thinking? Why is he acting the way that he is acting?"

That little moment of clarity can add a tremendous amount of understanding on our part and will help us build rapport with the other person very quickly. We don't necessarily have to agree with the person. But just looking at things from the other person's point of view is a big step forward.

If we want people to like and respect us, do the opposite of what comes naturally. See things from other's point of view. When we understand others, we are much more likely to be understood by them.

Week #1: Build Trust and Rapport Quickly
Principle #2: Look at Things from the Other Person's Point of View

---

Leadership Principle #3

Smile More

"The man who gives little with a smile gives more than the man who gives much with a frown." **– Jewish Proverb**

One thing I learned in high school and college was that if I wanted people to take me seriously, I had to have a serious, stern look.

I learned that if I was to be "in charge," I had to look unyielding.

Then I got into the real world and realized that the stern, unyielding look came across to others as a scowl. (Yes... Many of the things that we learn when we are young turn out to be bad practices when we get more experience.)

One morning, in my first job out of college, I came into the office and my boss pulled me aside and asked, "What's wrong? Are you okay?"

I told him that I was fine. However, he persisted. He just knew that I must have been having a bad day, and he was concerned.

I was finally able to convince him that I was happy. Later, though, I rethought the entire conversation. Was it possible that my stern look was causing people to think that I was mad or unapproachable?

I made a change that day. I began smiling more. Low and behold, people began smiling back.

Eventually, they even began to make small talk. It was amazing.

PEOPLE TEND TO RESPOND IN KIND WITH WHAT THEY SEE

I told this story to my class once, and one of my class members took it to heart. He went home that night, and when his wife met him, he smiled a very big grin at her.

She was so shocked, that she asked what had happened. He told her that nothing out of the ordinary had happened. He did tell her he was just glad to see her, and he was glad that she was his wife.

When he woke up the next morning, she had made him breakfast for the first time in two years. You can bet he is smiling more often today.

A BETTER OPEN-DOOR POLICY

Many managers and supervisors have an "open door policy," but because of the atmosphere that they create, no one ever walks through the open door.

When someone has a problem or needs help, they walk up to the door, just about to walk in, and they see the negative countenance.

Most people just turn around and decide to come back later.

A neutral expression can be just as unconstructive.

People don't like to guess about whether someone that they work for or work with is in a good mood or bad mood. A genuine smile can do a lot for you and for the people around you because it will make you more approachable.

Smiles are also contagious. One well placed smile can go along way to improving morale and building rapport.

Week #1: Build Trust and Rapport Quickly
Principle #3: Smile More

Leadership Principle #4

Make an Effort to Remember Names

"A person's name is to that person, the sweetest most important sound in any language."
– Dale Carnegie

Have you ever been in one of those situations where you run into someone that you have met before and can't remember that person's name? It can be an awkward situation for both you and the other person.

When we remember someone's name, we're telling him, "You're important." Therefore, when we forget a person's name, we may leave the opposite impression.

Do you want great service at a restaurant? Call the waitress by name when you place your order.

Want to be the center of influence at a party?

Introduce people you just met to others at the party.

People love to hear their own name. In fact, Dale Carnegie said that "a person's name is to that person, the sweetest most important sound in any language."

One of the first things we teach in our High Impact Leaders course is a simple way to remember names. It is a technique that is so simple that many people in a class of 25 will be able to recall the first and last names of every single person in the classroom within the first hour of class.

(Access a free mini-course teaching this technique at https://www.leadersinstitute.com/remember-names)

In 1988, Harvey Mackay wrote a book called *Swim with the Sharks without Being Eaten Alive*, and he wanted to get it published. When he found a publisher that would talk to him, he had the audacity to request that the first edition print 100,000 copies.

The publisher thought that Mackay was nuts. No publisher would print that many copies of a book written by a first-time author. Then Mackay pulled out his Rolodex and showed the publisher how he knew over 6,500 people on a first name basis, and he consciously kept in contact with each one.

The publisher took a chance and ended up selling over 300,000 copies of the first book.

Harvey Mackay used his ability to remember people – remember their names to build his million-dollar company. Then, he used the same relationships to build his writing and speaking career.

You can do the same thing. If you want to be a good people person, focus on remembering names. They will feel more important because you remembered, and they will think more of you as well.

Week #1: Build Trust and Rapport Quickly
Principle #4: Make an Effort to Remember Names.

Leadership Principle #5

Avoid Placing the Burden of Your Problems onto Other People

"A prudent man will think more important what fate has conceded to him, than what it has denied him." **– Baltasar Gracian**

Have you ever known someone who, after any setback, had an excuse and typically laid the blame elsewhere?

I'm ashamed to say that at one point in my life, I was one of those people.

- The economy is down.
- The economy is bad.
- My manger shows favoritism to her pets.
- That was my coworker's fault. I had nothing to do with it!

I had one for any occasion.

Luckily, at one point in my career, I had a good friend that sat me down and said, "You can continue to come up with more excuses, or you can use less energy by just solving the problem."

ALL YOUR MISTAKES HAVE ONE THING IN COMMON

It hit me like a ton of bricks. It wasn't the economy or my manager. It wasn't my coworker who was causing me to fail. I realized that every mistake or problem that had ever occurred in my life had one common variable. -- ME!

At that point, I took a good look at myself. I looked at some of the mistakes I had made and asked myself, how can I avoid making the same mistake again?

I started to use every obstacle as a learning experience. Don't get me wrong, I still make excuses on occasion, but they are few and far between, and they no longer define me.

Since I made that conscious decision, my career has really taken off. There are some people out there who make themselves feel better by bringing other people down.

They revel in their ability to know who had a heart attack, who is getting divorced, who is stealing office supplies, and more. The more they can bring other people down, the better that they feel.

MISERY LOVES COMPANY

Unfortunately, when the gossip starts, it's easy to get caught up in it.

My fourth-grade teacher, Mrs. Lofton used to say, ***"Misery loves company."*** So just one person in your office with this type of mentality can cause the morale and team atmosphere in your office to drop like a stone.

Good leaders are the ones who stop this type of behavior in its tracks by just refusing to participate and standing up for coworkers who aren't there to defend themselves. If you want to be a great leader, avoid placing the burden of your problems onto other people.

Week #1: Build Trust and Rapport Quickly
Principle #5: Avoid Placing the Burden of Your Problems onto Other People

---

Leadership Principle #6

Assume Responsibility for Clear Communication

"The greatest problem in communication is the illusion that it has been accomplished."
– Daniel W. Davenport

Communication is a two-way street. For communication to be successful, we must have both a successful speaker **and** an effective listener. If either party is not present, miscommunication may occur. However, there are things we can do to reduce miscommunication.

For example, I used to work for a man who had been extremely successful in business. I was fairly young, but I had a number of great ideas that I frequently told him about. I noticed, however, that when I shared many of my ideas, he discounted them immediately.

Sometimes, I would leave his office upset and tell some of my coworkers how he wouldn't even listen to me. Often, when these coworkers agreed with my ideas, they would bring them back up to the boss later.

For some reason, he always seemed to be more open to the ideas when he heard them a second time.

I realized that we had a communication problem, so I learned that if I wanted my ideas to be heard, I needed support from my coworkers.

WHEN LEADERS IDENTIFY A COMMUNICATION PROBLEM, THEY FIGURE OUT WAYS TO FIX IT

Many times, I would plant the seed with the boss and then tell someone else the idea. Often, the idea would be implemented with a few weeks.

We all listed to each other at different levels depending on circumstances that are present. The leader is the person who takes into account these circumstances and the character of the listener in order to make sure that the communication occurred.

For instance, if you know you are communicating with a person who is not really detail oriented, and you give instructions verbally just once, you have a very small chance that the person will follow through on your instructions. So, for that person, it might be a good idea to follow up with a text, phone call, or email. Or, you might have to send some written instructions to the person.

Regardless of how you follow up, if you want to ensure that the communication occurs, you must go above and beyond the call of duty.

To be a great leader, take responsibility for clear communication.

Week #1: Build Trust and Rapport Quickly
Principle #6: Assume Responsibility
for Clear Communication

Leadership Principle #7

Practice Good Listening Skills

"A good listener is not only popular everywhere, but after a while he gets to know something."
– Wilson Mizner

My first year in sales, I read a book about how to be a good listener. The book said that if I wanted to be a good listener, I should make eye contact, say "Uh huh" a lot, and then paraphrase what the person just said.

I couldn't wait to go on my next sales call. I asked my prospect a question, made solid eye contact, said "Uh huh" a lot, and then said the words I read in the book over and over... "So, what I hear you saying is..."

Take it from first-hand experience; this type of listening does NOT work. My prospect looked at me like I was from Pluto and said, "If you're having trouble keeping up, maybe I should go a little slower."

I was pretty embarrassed, and when I got back to my office, I quickly tossed the book into the trash.

DON'T LOOK FOR LISTENING "TECHNIQUES"

Don't look for techniques on how to listen better. The people who are great listeners do so because they want to be great listeners, not because they learned the latest "technique" to trick people into thinking that they are listening when they aren't.

I've noticed that there are about four different levels of listening.

THE FOUR LEVELS OF LISTENING

The lowest level of listening is to completely **Ignore** the speaker. We all fall into this trap from time to time, such as when we are in a boring meeting and our mind wanders.

The second level of listening is when we **Pretend** to listen, but we are really just looking for an opportunity to end the conversation or change the subject.

The third level of listening is when we **Selectively** listen (mainly out of self-interest.) When we listen at this level, we will practically ignore the other person unless they are talking about something that directly concerns us.

Selective listeners will sometimes listen just enough to form an opinion or a rebuttal. They tend to interrupt a lot and give advice.

When we move into this level of listening, a lot of times, we do so to speed up the listening process. But for the most part, this type of listening can slow down the communication process giving us a negative result.

The highest level of listener is the **Attentive or Focused** listener. This person ignores all distractions and focuses totally on the speaker.

In any given conversation, we will typically slip from one of these types of listening levels to another. The key is to get our minds off ourselves and onto the other person.

If we are genuinely interested in the other person – if we really care about the other person – we will automatically spend more time in the focused listening level.

Week #1: Build Trust and Rapport Quickly
Principle #7: Be a Good Listener

Week #1 Recap: Building Trust and Rapport

Day 1: **Avoid criticizing and complaining.**

Day 2: **Look at things from the other person's point of view.**

Day 3: **Smile more.**

Day 4: **Make an effort to remember names.**

Day 5: **Avoid placing the burden of your problems onto other people.**

Day 6: **Assume responsibility for clear communication.**

Day 7: **Practice good listening skills.**

Don't forget to download your FREE bonus pack: leadersinstitute.com/bonuspack

Week #2

Conflict Resolution Skills

Many of this week's principles will help you create a more positive outcome from negative situations.

These principles are excellent when used to calm an angry person or persuade people to see a different point of view. You may not convince the other person every time, but you should see more positive resolutions.

Keep in mind, that if we have not established solid trust by using the principles from last week, resolving conflicts can be much more difficult.

8.   Be proactive instead of reactive.

9. Be slow to anger—especially over petty issues.

10. Instead of telling people they are wrong, point out mistakes indirectly.

11. Look for some type of common ground as soon as possible.

12. If you find that you are in the wrong, admit it.

13. Admit one of your own poor decisions before pointing out a similar error by others.

14. Mend fences whenever possible.

Leadership Principle #8

Be Proactive Instead of Reactive.

"Good plans shape good decisions. That's why good planning helps to make elusive dreams come true." **– Lester R. Bittel**

George Bernard Shaw said, "The people who get on in this world are the people who get up and look for the circumstances they want, and, if they can't find them, make them."

That is great advice for any leader. People who wait for things to happen are always at least one step behind the people who make things happen.

I spent my first year as a manager constantly moving from one fire to the next. Once the stress became so unbearable, I did something that was entirely out of my comfort zone... I asked for help from my mentor.

I explained to him what an average day was for me. Then, after he stopped laughing, he asked me a few questions that just floored me.

First, he asked, "How much of your time do you spend planning?"

I tried to explain to him that I had a daily calendar, but he told me that a schedule was a good start but wasn't enough.

He then asked more questions, "Before you make a decision, do you first look for possible obstacles that could slow down implementation?"

My delayed answer told him all that he needed to know.

His final question was, "How much of your budget do you have set aside for training your people?"

He could tell by my blank stare that I had never thought of any of those things. Then, he gave me a piece of advice that I have found to be invaluable. He said that if I spent more time preparing and planning, then I could better control the outcome.

He was right.

IF YOU ARE CONSTANTLY PUTTING OUT FIRES, TRY BEING MORE PROACTIVE

Most managers and supervisors think that their job is to look for problems and then come in on their white horse to fix them.

The big challenge with this type of thinking is that once the problem presents itself, we've already lost time and money. The manager feels good about herself because she has an opportunity to put out a fire and become a hero. But every time this happens, we are teaching the people that work for us that it is okay to be sloppy. Why not? The boss will always come in and save us.

In order to help our people grow and reduce conflicts, let's be proactive versus reactive.

Week #2: Conflict Resolution
Principle #8: Be Proactive versus Reactive

Leadership Principle #9

Be Slow to Anger—Especially Over Petty Issues.

"Anger is always more harmful than the insult that caused it." **– Chinese Proverb**

Two men in Sacramento, Timothy Mann and Donald Bell, were both driving on Highway 50 one Sunday afternoon when Bell "cut-off" Mann. They yelled and cursed at each other, and when Mann exited the highway, Bell followed.

At a stoplight, they both got out of their cars to continue the altercation. Mann took a swing at Bell, and before his fist connected, Bell shot him in the head at point-blank range in front of his wife and son.

Two weeks later, at about the same time on Sunday, Bell returned to the scene and shot himself.

It's easy for us to look at these two grown men behaving in a despicable way and criticize their actions. But how many times have we gotten upset over issues just as trivial?

WHEN WE GET ANGRY, WE LOSE CONTROL

We must remember that when we get angry, we lose control. We may say or do things that we later regret.

When things don't go our way, or someone slights us, or circumstances turn against us, the natural human reaction is to get angry. The longer that we let it fester, the angrier we get. After a little bit of time, something that was very small in the beginning becomes huge as we play it over and over in our heads.

The worst thing that we can do at this point is to confront the person who has slighted us, because people tend to respond in kind to us. If we begin to get angry, the person we are communicating with will probably begin to get angry as well. The argument will quickly escalate.

PEOPLE TEND TO RESPOND IN-KIND

However, when people get angry with us, and we remain calm and collected, one of two things will happen. They may storm off, frustrated, because we didn't fight back. Or they will realize how foolish they appear and feel ashamed. Once people have a chance to vent, and the person that they are venting to remains calm and collected, they will typically cool down and begin to communicate more clearly. Remember, people respond in kind to what they see and hear.

Either way, we have avoided the negative consequences. So, if you want to keep long-lasting friendships, be slow to anger especially over petty issues.

Week #2: Conflict Resolution
Principle #9: Be Slow to Anger
Especially Over Petty Issues

Leadership Principle #10

Instead of Telling People They Are Wrong, Point Out Mistakes Indirectly.

"A person convinced against his will is of the same opinion still." **– Samuel Butler**

In Ben Franklin's autobiography, he wrote about how in his younger years, he made many enemies because he frequently corrected people publicly when they were wrong.

45

What he found was that although he was very convincing and had facts on his side, he rarely persuaded anyone that they were wrong.

"A man convinced against his will is
of the same opinion still."

To make things worse, he noticed that many of these men held grudges against him for years.

Ben Franklin learned from his mistakes. He developed several skills that we can use as well. When someone stated an opinion that was in error, he began to respond with phrases such as, "In many cases, I would probably feel the same as you about this. However, if the facts of the situation were different..."

He also came up with what salespeople now call the "Ben Franklin Close," in which he drew a line down the middle of a piece of paper. He would then ask the person who differed with him to tell him all the pros of his idea, and he wrote them on one side. He then asked for all the cons and wrote them on the other. The other person usually came to his conclusion by being a little more objective.

ASK QUESTIONS TO POINT OUT MISTAKES INDIRECTLY

One of the best ways to point out mistakes indirectly is to ask questions. Let me give you an example.

Let's say that you have a person who works for you who is constantly turning in reports after the requested deadline. You might start by giving clarification to your entire team about the importance of the deadline.

Then, if the person continues to turn in the information late, follow up with a question like, "I know that the team is focusing on getting the reports in early. How did you do with your report this week?"

Instead of getting angry, the person will typically try to offer some type of excuse.

When this happens, just follow up with one more question, "Yeah, I can understand how that would be a problem. What are you going to do this week to make sure that it doesn't cause a challenge for you again?"

If you use this type of questioning, the person is more likely to take responsibility for making sure that the activity gets completed properly. So, let's take a page from Ben Franklin's autobiography and never tell someone "you're wrong."

Week #2: Conflict Resolution
Principle #10: Point Out Mistakes Indirectly

Leadership Principle #11

Look for Some Type of Common Ground as Soon as Possible.

"A compromise is the art of dividing a cake in such a way that everyone believes he has the biggest piece."
- Ludwig Erhard

Even if you use every one of the principles in this book consistently, the occasional disagreement is inevitable. There are many ways to deal with disagreements but arguing with the other party is one sure way to guarantee that you will **not** persuade the other person.

49

When we argue, each side will begin to become defensive.

A PERSON WHO IS DEFENSIVE WILL VERY RARELY SEE THE LOGIC IN AN ARGUMENT

In 1787, George Washington and our founding fathers met in Philadelphia at the Constitutional Convention. Disputes arose frequently and compromise was essential. At one point in the process, Washington wrote, "*No morn ever dawned more favorable than ours did; and no day was every more clouded than the present!*"

One of the biggest disputes was whether to have representatives in the unicameral congress to be determined by equal representation among the states or to have the number of representatives be determined by the population of each state.

Of course, the smaller states wanted the former and the larger states wanted the latter. Eventually, a compromise was agreed to based on James Madison's suggestion that a bicameral legislation be created and Roger Sherman's suggestion that the House be determined by population and the Senate have equal representation.

That one instance of common ground led to the foundation of one of the most remarkable human governments to ever exist. The representatives of each of the states got to go back to their homes satisfied that they inked out a good deal for their fellow citizens.

FIND COMMON GROUND

If the goal is to persuade the other person, then it is a good idea to find some common ground.

Ask yourself a few questions.
- What about the two opinions is similar?

- What is some point that we can agree upon?
- What single thing can we both agree on?

I am not suggesting that you cave in, by the way –
far from it. What I am suggesting is tearing down
the defensive walls so that both parties can see a
logical conclusion.

When we can find common ground, the emotion
and defensiveness are somewhat diminished. At
this point, if we use some of the other principles
from this booklet to allow the other person to save
face if he is wrong. This will allow us to come to a
satisfactory conclusion.

So, when you feel an argument brewing, find some
common ground as soon as possible.

Week #2: Conflict Resolution
**Principle #11: Look for Some Type of
Common Ground as Soon as Possible**

Leadership Principle #12

If You Find that You Are in the Wrong, Admit It.

"It's easier to eat crow while it is still warm."
– Dan Heist

I once hired a consultant who had more natural talent in our business than I have ever seen. I invited him to sit in on a sales call that was worth about $32,000 worth of consulting.

(That was a HUGE contract for me at the time.)

Just before we walked into the door, I explained to my new consultant that this was a very big deal for me. I also explained that I had been working on it for some time. I told him that although he was there to watch and learn, if he had ideas that might help to feel free to bring them to me.

That was a big mistake.

I basically put someone with a lot of talent into a position where he was in way over his head and invited him to experiment.

Every time my potential customer asked me a clarifying question, I would explain the process in a little more detail. Then, immediately after I finished, my consultant-in-training would jump in and try to "save the deal."

I was very frustrated. My goal was to help this young person grow. However, since he had very little experience in consulting calls like this, he had no idea that his "help" was actually "hurting" the potential client. Our drive back to the office was very quiet. In my head, I was watching months of work go down the drain.

MY MISTAKE CAUSED THE ORIGINAL PROBLEM

I went over what I wanted to say to him many times in my head, but I just couldn't figure out how to say something that didn't sound really angry. Finally, I told him that, while I welcomed his input, his constant interruptions made it very difficult for me to help the customer.

I expected him to be apologetic. However, his reaction was quite different. He just said, "I only jumped in when I was sure that you were blowing the sale."

At that point, all my prepared verbiage went out the window. I exploded. I went on a tirade telling him that his 3-weeks of experience didn't make him an expert.

(I know... Not my best moment. This is also one of those moments that I have regretted for many years.)

When I was finished, I turned to my computer and ignored him the rest of the day. I knew I needed to apologize, but I let him leave without saying a word. He never came back.

WHEN YOU ARE WRONG, JUST ADMIT IT QUICKLY

If I had confessed MY mistake, instead of pointing out his, I probably could have helped him build a promising career.

Do you realize that if we were right just 51% of the time, we'd all be multi-gazillionaires? The truth is that we are wrong much more often than we are right. When you find yourself on the wrong side of the argument, be the bigger person and admit it.

Week #2: Conflict Resolution
Principle #12: If You Find That You are in The Wrong, Admit It

---

Leadership Principle #13

Admit One of Your Own Poor Decisions Before Pointing Out a Similar Error by Others.

"The only real mistake is the one from which we learn nothing."
- Henry Ford

In my early days of selling, my mentor was a lady named Sally Bartz. She had been an award-winning salesperson for one of the top training companies in the world for many years. The first day I met her, she told me that her job was to coach me to be a better salesperson. She said that from time to time she would point out some things to me where I could make improvements, and that she was only able to do this because she had already made every mistake imaginable. She knew what didn't work, so she could help me focus in the areas that did work.

She was very consistent. Anytime she saw me doing or saying something that could cost me potential sales, she would matter-of-factly say something like, "I remember back when I..." and she would tell me about a time when she had made a similar mistake. Her indirect coaching allowed me to save face, and it helped my career because I didn't have to make the same mistakes that she had made.

Did it work? You bet. Within three years, I was one of the top salespeople in the world for that company and had become a pretty good coach as well.

It's very easy to point out mistakes that others are making in an overt way. Most people do this. However, it takes a skilled mentor to point out mistakes in a way that lets the other person save face.

Letting people know how you have made a similar mistake first allows them to be more open minded about their own mistakes.

Week #2: Conflict Resolution
Principle #13: Admit One of your Own Poor Decisions before Pointing Out a Similar Mistake by Others

Leadership Principle #14

Mend Fences Whenever Possible.

"Never does the human soul appear so strong as when it forgoes revenge, and dares forgive an injury."
- E.H. Chapin

This principle sounds like common sense, but it's uncommon in practice. Many relationships have ended with one party feeling slighted by the other, and neither side being big enough to make amends. And the longer we wait, the more the problem festers.

Two managers were recently consulted about a very sticky problem that had surfaced. The senior manager offered a suggestion to the boss that sounded reasonable. However, the more junior manager disagreed. Then, in front of other staff members, he told everyone why the idea wouldn't work.

After a few weeks, the junior manager noticed that tasks that had usually been completed in a timely manner by the other manager were taking an unusually long time. He knew why. So, he pulled the other manager aside and offered an apology.

The senior manager's face got very crimson, and he exploded. He cursed. He screamed. The junior manager just let him vent and apologized again. The senior manager stopped, apologized for his outburst, and afterward, things pretty much went back to normal.

Realize that if the junior manager had apologized quickly, the outburst probably wouldn't have occurred. The longer that a problem or argument festers, the more damage will develop in the relationship. So, mend fences with those you have wronged, and do it quickly.

Week #2: Conflict Resolution
Principle #14: Mend Fences Whenever Possible

Week #2 Recap:
Conflict Resolution

Day 8: Be proactive instead of reactive.

Day 9: Be slow to anger—especially over petty issues.

Day 10: Instead of telling people they are wrong, point out mistakes indirectly.

Day 11: Look for some type of common ground as soon as possible.

Day 12: If you find that you are in the wrong, admit it.

Day 13: Admit one of your own poor decisions before pointing out a similar error by others.

Day 14: Mend fences whenever possible.

Don't forget to download your FREE bonus pack: leadersinstitute.com/bonuspack

Week #3
Gain Enthusiastic Cooperation from Others

Many of this week's principles will help you gain cooperation from others. The only way to get people to do things for you is to get them to WANT to do things for you.

Most people have an eager want to be accepted by others or want to be esteemed by their peers. So, if we can show people how what we want them to do will help them become more of a part of the team, then they will usually enthusiastically do what we ask.

These are the 7seven things that you can do to gain cooperation from others.

15. Acknowledge the importance of other people.

16. Show enthusiasm and energy.

17. Encourage and facilitate two-way conversations.

18. Ask other people's opinions.

19. Ask questions instead of giving orders.

20. Show sincere gratitude.

21. Give strength-centered compliments.

Leadership Principle #15

Acknowledge the Importance of Other People.

"The deepest principle in human nature is the craving to be appreciated." **– William James**

Most people have one defining need that very rarely gets satisfied. Many of us will move Heaven and Earth to satisfy this need. This one attribute is the single most motivating factor that leads to success. It is the need – the want – to feel important.

The person who can satisfy this need in others, the person who can sincerely make other people feel important, can be very influential and is typically regarded by others as a good leader.

WHAT MAKES YOU FEEL IMPORTANT?

In fact, you can tell a lot about an individual by what makes him feel important. My dad builds houses, and one of the most satisfying things to him is to complete a building and have others admire his work.

Al Capone got his feeling of being important from power and control.

Mother Teresa got her feeling of importance by helping the helpless.

There are usually two reasons why people do things. The reason we tell others... and the real reason.

When we give money to charity, do we really do it to help others or do we do it because of the satisfaction **we get** from helping others?

We feel important because we feel like we made a difference in someone else's life.

We you look around your office, you will see people from all walks of life who crave this feeling of importance. If any one of those people, all of the sudden, stopped doing their job, it would cause a lot of challenges for your company. Every single job that they do is important to the success of the company – to your success. Without them you couldn't do your job effectively.

When was the last time that you told them how important they were to you?

SHOW PEOPLE THAT YOU APPRECIATE THEM

One of my class members about ten years ago decided to use this principle with his sales assistant.

Actually, she was the assistant for five different salespeople – he was just one of the five. Her job was to put together marketing materials and, ultimately, their contracts when they sold a big deal.

During my class, this salesman realized that the work that this woman did for him was critical to him closing deals. (She was important to his success.) So, on his way into the office, he bought her a big container of popcorn and just put a sticky note on top of the can saying how much he appreciated her work.

When he gave it to her, she was shocked and surprised. However, she was also awfully grateful since he was the first person in years to treat her like an equal in the office.

When he came back to class the next week, he told us that she had taken the sticky note off the can and stuck it under the plastic protector that covered her desk so that she could see it every day.

I saw this man a couple of years later and asked him about the sales assistant. He told me that she is still there and still doing a fabulous job. He said, though, that she now has over a dozen of the sticky notes on her desk. She keeps each one.

Great leaders use this aspect of human nature to make people feel important. One way to be a great leader is to find some way every day to make the people around you feel important.

Week #3: Gain Enthusiastic Cooperation
Principle #15: Acknowledge the Importance of Other People

Leadership Principle #16

Show Enthusiasm and Energy.

"Enthusiasm is by far the highest paid quality on earth, probably because it is one of the rarest; yet it is one of the most contagious." **– Frank Bettger**

Have you ever noticed that the most successful people in just about any industry are the early risers? Ben Franklin called this group of people the "Six O'clock Club."

Franklin spent the first hour of his day planning the events of his day (to do this he invented the Franklin Planner) and reading. He often claimed that the first hour of his day was the most important.

How does this relate to raising your own energy level? We have a choice every morning when we wake up. Do I want to hit the snooze bar a few times, or do I want to put some energy and enthusiasm into my day?

Frank Bettger, in his book *How I Raised Myself from Failure to Success in Selling,* said that if he had to narrow down to one thing why he has been so successful, it would be enthusiasm.

ENTHUSIASM IS A SECRET TO SUCCESS

His enthusiasm was what moved him from a "second rate bush league making $25 a week" to the starting shortstop for the St. Louis Cardinals. His enthusiasm was also what transformed him from a washout in sales to the most successful insurance agent of his time.

Where did his enthusiasm come from?

He says that he didn't have any enthusiasm in the beginning, but he faked it. He acted like he was enthusiastic, and behold he was. **After a few successes, the enthusiasm came easy**.

SUCCESSFUL PEOPLE DO THINGS THAT OTHERS AVOID

You have the same choice in your own life. When a dirty job must be done, jump in with lots of enthusiasm and gusto. When you have a challenging project that no one else wants to do, you can use that project as an opportunity to get yourself noticed.

Everyone wants to be around people who are going somewhere. The person who sets out to enthusiastically get to the next level will attract tons of followers. Enthusiasm is contagious.

Take the advice of Franklin and Bettger and raise your energy level and the people around you will stop and take notice.

Week #3: Gain Enthusiastic Cooperation
Principle #16: Show Enthusiasm and Energy

Leadership Principle #17

Encourage and Facilitate Two-Way Conversation.

"Education is a kind of continuing dialogue, and a dialogue assumes, in the nature of the case, different points of view." - **Robert Hutchins**

Oprah Winfrey was the most successful daytime TV star of all time and is still one of the most influential people in America. When she promoted a book on her television show, it would typically be on the bestseller list within a week.

However, I'd wager that Ms. Winfrey's success would have been far less dramatic if she had used her show to lecture her audience for an hour a day.

One of the characteristics of her show that made her so influential was the fact that she created a one-on-one dialogue with her guests as well as with her audience. Her audience, and her influence, grew year after year.

CREATE TWO-WAY CONVERSATIONS TO IMPROVE COMMUNICATION

We can learn from her success. You too can have more influence over others if you create two-way communication.

One of the most common complaints I hear from front-line employees is that top management does not take their ideas seriously and does not address their concerns. Many companies today have a top-down communication in place that can stifle creativity and build resentment in front-line employees.

Many of these employees have ideas that could revolutionize the company, but far too often, the ideas are overlooked because the people at the top are too focused on the status quo.

IDEAS FROM YOUR FRONT-LINE WORKERS CAN MAKE MILLIONS

Herb Peterson was a McDonald's franchise holder in 1972 when he had an idea to add breakfast to the menu. At that time, McDonald's was just a hamburger place without a lot of additional items, and no one would want to go to a hamburger place for breakfast.

Herb went ahead and crafted a Teflon circle in his garage to be able to easily cook eggs Benedict on a hamburger grill, and he took the idea to the McDonald's headquarters in Chicago. Today, it's estimated that McDonald's sells about $4 billion worth of breakfast every year.

Those dialogues that we create with the people who work for us can provide us with valuable information – both good and bad. This information is critical in helping us make solid decisions in the marketplace.

If you want to influence others in a positive way, take a lesson from Oprah and McDonald's and create dialogues rather than monologues.

Week #3: Gain Enthusiastic Cooperation
Principle #17: Encourage and Facilitate Two-Way Communication

Leadership Principle #18

Ask Other People's Opinions.

"I have opinions of my own -- strong opinions -- but I don't always agree with them." **– George W. Bush**

One of my class members was a project manager for a commercial construction company. On the last day of a big job he had been working on, he noticed that one of the sub-contractors had bricked the doorframe the wrong way.

To make matters worse, the architect and the client were expected later that afternoon to conduct the final walk through. He knew that if he had to call the mason back out, it would take at least another day and would cost a few thousand dollars.

Since he was in a bind, he called all the foremen together and asked what they thought he could do to fix the problem. One of them asked to borrow the crane and a skill saw and beveled the rocks by hand. The work was done so well that the architect sent a picture of the building in to be judged for an award from the American Institute of Architects.

ASK THE OPINOIN OF YOUR EXPERTS TO GAIN INSIGHT

When we are under the gun, most of us want to take control and begin to order people around.

Since time is short, we want to quicken the pace by just telling people what to do instead of asking them their opinion. When we do this, though, we are often missing an opportunity to gain great insights from the people who are on the front line.

One of the hardest things for young people to realize when they get their first leadership position is that they don't know everything yet. When we are young, we think that our formal education taught us everything we'd ever need to know.

When we get into the real world and realize that we don't know it all yet, we want to **make sure that no one ever finds out**.

TO BECOME AN EXPERT, ASK FOR HELP FROM OTHER EXPERTS

The best thing to do in this situation is to admit that you need help or more information. Most people around you will respect you more.

Captain Christopher J. Courtney in his article called "The Successful Lieutenant" said it well, "It is a cardinal error for a lieutenant to be a 'know-it-all.' Nothing turns off the troops faster or brings down morale more than a know-it-all lieutenant... Admitting to your platoon sergeant that you do not know something is not a sign of weakness, it is a sign of honesty."

WISDOM COMES BY GAINING FROM THE EXPERIENCE OF OTHERS

When we take the time to ask those around us who have years more of experience in the industry what they think, we can gain great wisdom.

In addition, when we implement some of the great ideas from the people who work for us, they will jump into the change feet first. **People love a world that they help create**. If you want to gain buy-in from others, ask for their opinion and really listen to their responses. You may find that the ideas they come up with to be very valuable.

Week #3: Gain Enthusiastic Cooperation
Principle #18: Ask Other People's Opinions

28 WAYS TO INFLUENCE PEOPLE

Leadership Principle #19

Ask Questions Instead of Giving Orders.

"Never tell people how to do things. Tell them what you want them to achieve and they will surprise you with their ingenuity." **– Gen. George S. Patton**

David was a recent graduate of engineering school and was in his first supervisory position on a construction project. Many of the men who worked with and for him had 10, 15, and even 20 years of experience.

David's job was to interpret the designs from the architect and get his crew to implement the designs. So, every morning, he would meet with the superintendents and foremen and tell them what they were to do that day.

After a few months, David began to realize that the ideas he brought to the crew typically were either taking a long time to implement or had to be reworked.

David's general contractor realized what was going on and explained to him that the crew resented being ordered around on the jobsite. He asked David to begin to ask for the advice of his superintendents and foremen rather than dictating to them.

The difference was like night and day. David began drawing up alternative plans and bringing them to the crew. He would ask their opinion, and nine times out of ten his original idea was the popular choice. The other 10% of the time, David learned valuable insights about design and construction. Things he could have never learned in school. Rework dropped dramatically.

When we order people to do things, they will resent us for telling them what to. Even if there is a great deal of trust, the person being ordered around will typically follow through out of compliance versus cooperation.

However, when we ASK people to do things for us, they will usually respond in a much more positive way. You can have similar results if you ask questions instead of giving orders.

Week #3: Gain Enthusiastic Cooperation
Principle #19: Ask Questions Instead of Giving Orders

Leadership Principle #20

Show Sincere Gratitude.

"God gave you a gift of 86,400 seconds today. Have you used one to say, 'thank you?'" **- William A. Ward**

In 1997, The Australian Institute of Family Studies published a paper called "Reasons for Divorce." It said that the #1 cause of divorce was communication problems resulting in one or both spouses feeling unappreciated.

I think that if someone did a survey of why people left their jobs, feeling unappreciated would rank very high on that list as well.

MOST PEOPLE ARE STARVING FOR APPRECIATION

We wouldn't dream of letting children (or employees) go for days without food, but we'll let them go years without something just as important, the feeling of being appreciated.

A simple kind word of appreciation is one of the simplest ways to build trust, gain cooperation, and anchor positive behavior in others.

A friend of mine had a staff of appraisers who were compensated for the number of appraisals that they wrote each week. After a few years, he noticed that the number of appraisals had increased, but quality was suffering. He was personally spending a great deal of time rechecking flawed documents. One day at a staff meeting, he publicly complimented one of the appraisers who had consistently provided flawless documents.

The appraiser received the appreciation with a smile and a blush, and my friend noticed that in the next few weeks, her work improved even more.

As a side benefit, within weeks, the overall quality of **everyone's** documents went up as well. He continued to compliment the improvements, and quality continued to rise.

What he realized was that for years, he had taken the people that worked for him for granted. He assumed that their paycheck was appreciation enough.

As he began to show each person how much he appreciated them, the quality of their work improved. Another benefit was that his job as the president of the company became easier and easier as well.

If you want to see growth in the people around you, then show them how much you appreciate them and watch the morale of your organization grow.

Week #3: Gain Enthusiastic Cooperation
Principle #20: Show Sincere Gratitude

Leadership Principle #21

Give Strength Centered Compliments.

"The life of many a person could probably be changed if someone would only make him feel important."
– Dale Carnegie

In our modern society, the art of giving people a sincere compliment has gone the way of the vinyl record or the Model T. You come across them occasionally, but they are few and far between.

I have asked hundreds of different audiences across the country why they think that we don't give as many compliments as we probably should (or receive the number of compliments that we probably deserve.) In response, I have heard every answer under the sun. But what I find most often is that we are mainly too self-centered and too busy to take the time to give a sincere compliment to our fellow human being.

A GOOD COMPLIMENT IS THE OPPOSITE OF FLATTERY

There is also a negative connotation about giving compliments to people. We think of people who give compliments as brown-nosers or kiss-asses. In the modern era, we have confused a sincere compliment with flattery. To most people they are one and the same.

In addition, men are also less inclined to give compliments to female coworkers out of fear of being accused of harassment.

With all these challenges to overcome, most people just don't bother to compliment one another now. It's easier just to keep to ourselves.

A GOOD LEADER CAN USE COMPLIMENTS TO SET YOURSELF APART FROM THE CROWD

You can compliment people on what they have. A compliment like this would be something like "Nice tie."

You can compliment people on what they do. "Thanks for turning in the report early," is an example.

However, each of these types of compliments has a chance of being seen as insincere.

However, if you give the people around you a compliment based on a strength of character that you notice in them, the compliment will always be seen as sincere.

Give them a strength-centered compliment and their confidence will grow. You will also be well thought of by that person.

To do this, instead of complimenting them on what they do, look for the strength or the character trait that allowed them to do the thing that you are admiring.

For instance, what allowed the person to get the report completed early? It could be that the person has a great work ethic or is detail oriented or is a great time manager. If you compliment her on one of these characteristics, then the compliment will mean a whole lot more to the person.

"I may not mention this enough, but I just wanted to tell you how much I admire your work ethic. You are one of the few people who consistently turns in the reports before the deadline every time. I really appreciate that about you."

A strength-centered compliment will boost the confidence of your coworkers faster than anything else that you can do.

Week #3: Gain Enthusiastic Cooperation
Principle #21: Give Strength-Centered Compliments

Week #3 Recap:
Gain Cooperation from People

Day 15:   Acknowledge the importance of other people.

Day 16:   Show enthusiasm and energy.

Day 17:   Encourage and facilitate two-way conversations.

Day 18:   Ask other people's opinions.

Day 19:   Ask questions instead of giving orders.

Day 20:   Show sincere gratitude.

Day 21:   Give strength-centered compliments.

Don't forget to download your FREE bonus pack: leadersinstitute.com/bonuspack

Week #4

Build the Next Generation of Leaders

The principles in the next section can help build the levels of trust and respect from others...

Many of this week's principles will help you gain the trust and respect from people around you. As the levels of trust and respect increase, your influence over others will grow. The trust and respect will result from the "Win/Win" relationships that you have already built by using the earlier principles.

22. Establish solid trust before offering advice.

23. Keep promises... even small ones.

24. Be enthusiastic about the success of others.

25. Recognize the potential in others and help them achieve it.

26. Catch people doing things right.

27. Praise the baby steps.

28. Go out of your way for people.

Leadership Principle #22

Establish Solid Trust Before Offering Advice.

"Trust men, and they will be true to you; treat them greatly and they will show themselves great."
– Ralph Waldo Emerson

The term "constructive criticism" is an oxymoron.

Think about it... When was the last time someone gave you constructive criticism and you responded with the following?

"Thank you so much for pointing out that mistake for me! If you hadn't said something, I would have just continued to screw that up. Thank you so much."

I know, I'm being a bit sarcastic, but it proves a point. Anytime we criticize someone, that person will always hold some resentment against us.

Can we point out the mistakes of others without resentment? Yes, but we must have their solid trust, and they must know that our only concern is their welfare.

EVERY RELATIONSHIP HAS VALUE

Picture your relationships with others as a check registry. Anytime you have said something positive to or done something positive for the person, add a deposit into the account.

Anytime you have said something negative to or done something negative against that person, register a withdrawal.

When we use the principles in the book, we build a positive trusting relationship with people, so we have a positive balance in this account. However, if we have violated these principles, then our relationship bank account may be way overdrawn.

We'll probably need to make more deposits before trying to influence these people or change their behavior.

THE AMOUNT OF INFLUENCE THAT WE HAVE DEPENDS ON THE LEVEL OF TRUST THAT WE HAVE

When people trust us, they are more likely to want to accept our advice and direction. Without that trust, though, our message, no matter how good it is, will fall on deaf ears.

I was walking in downtown Chicago a short time ago, and a street preacher was standing on the corner yelling, "Jesus saves!" I remember thinking, "What a nut." A couple of weeks later, I was in church and my preacher said something very similar. This time I was sure he was telling the truth.

The only difference between the two messages was the relationship that I had with the messenger.

Maintain a positive balance in your relationship accounts before offering constructive comments.

Week #4: Developing Leaders Around You
Principle #22: Establish Solid Trust before Offering Advice

Leadership Principle #23

Keep Promises...
Even Small Ones.

"Character is much easier kept than recovered."
- Thomas Paine

A person who breaks his word on little things is also likely to break his word on bigger things too.

Wes Zimmerman, author of *Perception of a Difference*, put it very clearly when he wrote, "It has been my experience that people possessing high integrity are honest in little things and big ones.

109

They are honest with themselves. They tend to think about what they are going to say before they say it. Above all, they do these things consistently. Their consistency earns my trust."

In contrast when someone breaks a promise, even a little one, it shows their character. They will tend to shade the truth and quote things out of context.

Once this character flaw is noticed, it is very difficult to gain back that trust that is lost.

When promises, even little ones, are kept consistently over time, the leader develops a level of trust with the people that he or she interacts with.

Brian Tracy, a famous speaker and trainers says that, "The glue that holds all relationships together -- including the relationship between the leader and the led is trust, and trust is based on integrity."

So, if you want to strengthen your integrity and build solid trust with your team, make sure to keep your promises.

Week #4: Developing Leaders Around You
Principle #23: Keep Promises, Even Small Ones

Leadership Principle #24

Be Enthusiastic about the Success of Others.

"Leaders don't create followers. They create more leaders." **- Tom Peters**

One common trait of great leaders is that they build other leaders along the way. Zig Ziglar said for years that if you help enough people become more successful, you can't help but become successful yourself.

This is true in our families, in our work environment, and also in our recreation.

For instance, one of the reason's Phil Jackson became one of the most successful basketball coaches of all time is that he was increasingly enthusiastic about the success of his players.

Michael Jordan believed that this was so important, that he refused to play for any other coach. Jackson has 8 NBA Championship rings as a coach. And in 1998 after his sixth championship, he told *Cigar Aficionado Magazine*, "It's normal for people to want more credit for success than is due them, yet the reality is that our championships were won on the court by Michael Jordan, Scottie Pippen, the other players and the coaching staff."

Three years later, he had moved to a new team, this time without Jordan and Pippen,

Did he take credit this time? Nope. In fact, just the opposite. He told USA Today, "It's incredible to be in this position as a coach," said Jackson. "Everything revolves around the team and the staff... I've been in the right spot and fortunate enough to have players who put me in this position."

Great players are attracted to Jackson because he builds great leaders, and you can too if you are as enthusiastic about their success as you are your own.

Week #4: Developing Leaders Around You
Principle #24: Be Enthusiastic about the Success of Others

Leadership Principle #25

Recognize the Potential in Others and Help Them Achieve It.

"Treat people as if they were what they should be, and you help them become what they are capable of becoming." **– Johann von Goethe**

For the past 20 years, The Leader's Institute ® instructors have helped people gain confidence in becoming effective leaders by pointing out strengths in our class members that they may not even recognize in themselves.

William James, the father of modern psychology, said that in a person's entire lifetime, he will only tap into 10% of his potential. Psychologists call this untapped potential our "blind spots."

OUR JOB AS LEADERS IS TO HELP MINIMIZE THE BLIND SPOTS IN OTHERS

When we recognize potential in others, we need to encourage them to tap into that potential.

When I was in college, I had a part time job facilitating after-school care for kids. I noticed that when I scolded or threatened the kids, they tested me even more. This was my first real position of authority, and the kids were showing me that they were really in charge.

I had to think fast, so I pulled one of the boys aside and asked him if he wanted to be my sheriff. I told him that if he wanted to be in authority that he had to help me by setting the example. It worked like a charm.

Once he was on my side, the other leaders in the group began to work with me rather than against me. As the year went on, these "problem" kids become some of the most responsible in the whole group.

This process works well with adults too. My files are full of letters from managers who came into their own shortly after getting that first big promotion.

OFTEN, BEING RECOGNIZED BY A LEADER IS THE CATALYST FOR NEW LEADERSHIP

All they needed was someone to believe in them. A boss, mentor, or supervisor saw potential in them.

119

Then, the confidence that they had grew even more dramatically when others see this confidence in them as well.

Don't discount people because they have a few rough edges. Instead, look for the strengths that they have and help them grow even more in those areas.

People tend to live up to the expectations that others set for them, so set your standards high and encourage others to reach them.

Week #4: Developing Leaders Around You
Principle #25: Recognize the Potential in Others and Help Them Achieve It

Leadership Principle #26

Catch People Doing Things Right.

"People ask for criticism, but they only want praise."
- W. Somerset Maugham

One of the best coaches that I have ever been associated with was Coach Gary Gaines, who was the linebacker coach at my college. He also had a book and movie made about him called *Friday Night Lights*.

121

What makes him Such a great coach is that he is a very mild-mannered person, but when he caught someone doing the right thing, he enthusiastically called attention to it. I still remember specific plays that I made in college because Coach Gaines would always give an immediate pat on the back. Then later, when we reviewed the film, he would show the great plays over and over again so that everyone saw them.

The other strength that Coach Gaines had was the way he made corrections and pointed out mistakes. Rather than saying, "Staneart, you missed two tackles," he called attention to the mistakes as a team. The TEAM missed six tackles. He let us save face.

In the few years that I played for him, he developed three players who played professional football and one who has been an all-pro every year he played.

MOST MANAGERS CALL ATTENTION TO MISTAKES

Most managers use what Ken Blanchard calls the "Leave Alone, Zap" method of coaching. They leave their direct reports alone until they make a mistake, and then they come by and "Zap" them to make corrective action.

This type of management style makes it to where the manager becomes the merchant of death in that the only time the direct reports get coaching is when they get hammered.

A better way of managing and coaching people is to look for the things that they are doing right and reinforce those things.

Show encouragement and help them strengthen those things that they are already doing well.

If we catch people doing things wrong, their focus is on the mistake. If we catch people doing things right, their focus is on their success. We get more of what we focus on most.

Week #4: Developing Leaders Around You
Principle #26: Catch People Doing Things Right

Leadership Principle #27

Praise the Baby Steps.

"Praise is like sunlight to the human spirit: we cannot flower and grow without it." **- Jess Lair**

Parents know that it takes patience, encouragement, and consistent action to teach a baby to walk. The baby takes one step and the parents cheer.

She falls down, the parents say, "That's OK. You can do it!"

The baby walks just a few feet, and she's a champion.

Why don't we use the same encouragement for our employees and coworkers?

DON'T LOOK FOR PERFECTION RIGHT AWAY. LOOK FOR IMPROVEMENT.

Most managers constantly call attention to the mistakes of their employees. Then they wonder why they must constantly look over the shoulders of their people. The secret to being a good manager is that whatever you call attention to, you get more of.

So, instead of pointing out the mistake, point out the improvement in the right direction.

If we want to build great leaders, we must help build their confidence as they gain experience. Call attention to their successes no matter how small these successes seem to be. When we do that, we are anchoring the positive behavior that they are exhibiting.

Want to change behavior? Try calling attention to someone's mistake indirectly, and then watch to see how the behavior changes.

When you catch that person doing things the right way, praise the improvement. Chances are that you'll begin to see this behavior more consistently.

Praise improvements in the right direction, and you'll build strong leaders around you.

Week #4: Developing Leaders Around You
Principle #27: Praise the Baby Steps

Leadership Principle #28

Go Out of Your Way for People.

"To lead the people, walk behind them." **- Lao-Tzu**

Joe Girard is the Guinness World Record holder for selling cars, because he constantly goes out of his way for his customers.

For instance, if his customers ever need service on their car, Girard personally represents them when they come into the service department, and sometimes, pays for the work himself. Every one of his customers (and there are thousands) receives a special card from him every month. It may be a St. Patrick's Day card in March or a Thanksgiving card in November, but they hear from him every month. He has hundreds of things that he does in which he goes out of his way to make sure his customers are satisfied, and most are repeat buyers and refer friends to him.

LEADERS GO THE EXTRA MILE

When we go out of our way for someone, when we do something above and beyond the call of duty, we are creating a memorable impression upon that person.

Harvey Mackay once had a friend relay a story about a colleague that called him at 2:00 AM desperate because he needed $20,000 or he would lose his business. This friend told Mackay that if his own business had been in trouble, he couldn't think of more than a couple of people he could call for help.

Mackay replied that he could name 50 people that he could call. Mackay has those relationships because he has gone to bat for each of those 50 people when they needed help.

By going the extra mile, his network of people who absolutely trust him is huge.

If you want relationships like that, go out of your way for people.

Week #4: Developing Leaders Around You
Principle #28: Go Out of Your Way for People

28 WAYS TO INFLUENCE PEOPLE

Bonus Principle
Leadership Principle #29

Always Give Something Extra

"Under promise; over deliver." **– Tom Peters**

There is a donut store in my neighborhood owned by a little oriental lady who is an expert at maximizing word-of-mouth advertising.

The first time I walked through her doors, she greeted me with a warm smile thanked me over and over for coming in, and gave me a fresh, hot donut hole to eat while I waited.

She had a whole store full of people but treated each one as if he or she were the only person in the world at that moment.

As I left the store with my order, I peeked into the box and found two extra donuts. I assumed that she had made a mistake. However, when I went back a couple of months later, she greeted me saying that I was her good customer and again I got more than I ordered.

When it happened the first time, I didn't tell a lot of people, but when I realized that that was her way of doing business, I told many people.

You can do the same in your business. Under promise and over deliver and the customer will always be happy.

When I conduct sales training, I promise a 10% increase in sales. When my clients receive a 40%, 50%, or even 60% increase, they are delighted, and they tell more people.

If you want to increase word-of-mouth advertising, always give a little extra.

BONUS PRINCIPLE
Principle #29: Always Give Something Extra

Week #4 Recap:
Developing Other Leaders

Day 22:   **Establish solid trust before offering advice.**

Day 23:   **Keep promises... even small ones.**

Day 24:   **Be enthusiastic about the success of others.**

Day 25:   **Recognize the potential in others and help them achieve it.**

Day 26:   **Catch people doing things right.**

Day 27:   **Praise the baby steps.**

Day 28:   **Go out of your way for people.**

Bonus: **Always give something extra.**

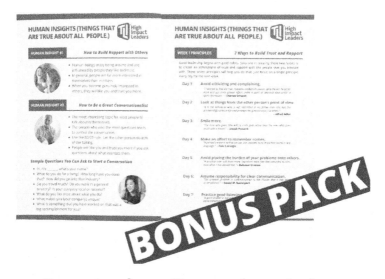

Reminder: Download the Bonus Pack!

Download at leadersinstitute.com/bonuspack

The first time I read a book about people skills, I realized that the principles written in the book made a lot of sense. Then, the next day, everything I read was a distant memory.

It wasn't until I made a conscious attempt to apply the principles from that book that I began to see results.

Every principle you have just read is time tested and 100% effective if used consistently. You can leverage the time you have spent reading this book by doing the following:

1. Read the book again over a 28-day period and **focus on just one principle per day** until the principle becomes second nature for you.

2. One of the best ways to increase the application of this material is if you get a friend or a group of coworkers together to follow the process with you.

3. Attend **High Impact Leaders** and receive personal coaching on using these principles and developing other leadership skills. For details, visit leadersinstitute.com

4. If you would like us to deliver a workshop for your company, call our office at (800) 872-7830 or email us at info@leadersinstitute.com.

Made in the USA
Monee, IL
22 April 2021